Nemo wanders too far away and is captured by a human diver! Marlin and his new friend Dory go into dangerous waters to look for clues that will help them find Nemo. Keep an eye out for these dangerous-looking sharks skulking about in the underwater minefield. Will Marlin and Dory make it through safely?

Bruce

Chum

Anchor

A basking shark

A sand shark

A whale shark

A tiger shark

Nemo is placed into a fish tank. As it turns out, the diver who caught him is actually a dentist who loves fish! But life in an aquarium is not much fun. Help Nemo and the other fish in the tank pass the time by finding all these things in the dentist's waiting room:

Dentists' Daily newspaper

A tooth mug

A fish painting

Swedish fish

Fish crackers

A fish lunch box

A rainbow fish

There is an address on a diver's mask Marlin and Dory found near the sub: "P. Sherman, 42 Wallaby Way, Sydney." But how will they get there when they can barely read? Some helpful moonfish make quite an "impression" by pointing the pair in the right direction. Can you help Marlin and Dory spot these other impressive moonfish signs?

"Swordfish"

"Octopus"

"Shark"

"Sea turtle"

"Starfish"

"Lobster"

"Whale"

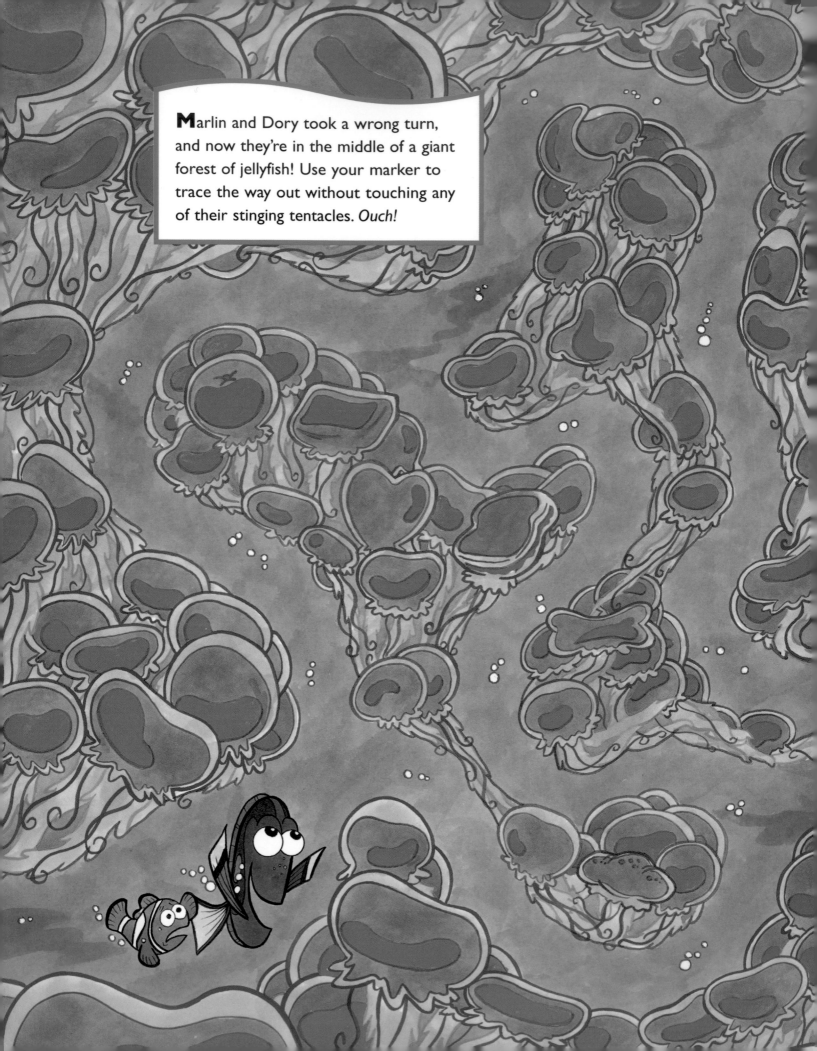

Marlin and Dory took a wrong turn, and now they're in the middle of a giant forest of jellyfish! Use your marker to trace the way out without touching any of their stinging tentacles. *Ouch!*

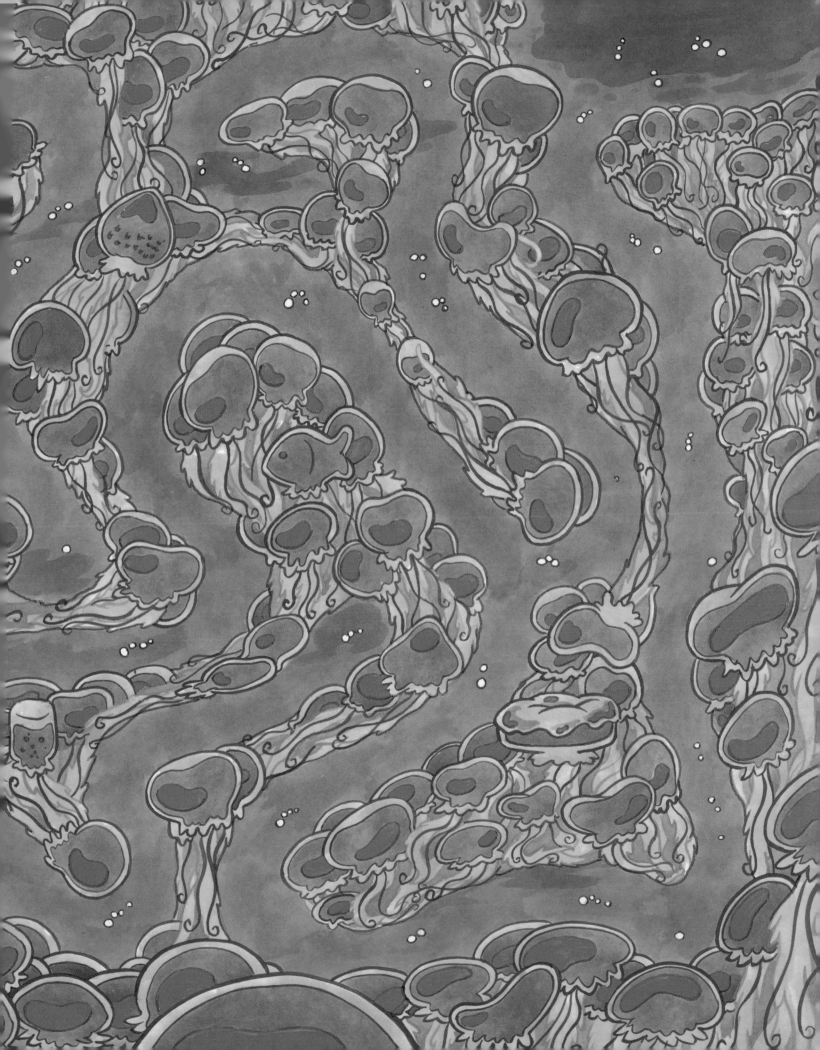

Whoa! After escaping the jellyfish forest, Marlin and Dory meet up with a group of friendly turtles, including Crush and his son Squirt. They're all cruising down the East Australian Current, which should drop them off right by Sydney! See if you can scope out Crush, Squirt, and these other gnarly, shelled dudes!

Squirt

Crush

Flora

Checkers

Noelle

Target

Sydney

Pelé

Once they get to Sydney, a nice pelican named Nigel takes Marlin and Dory to the dentist's office—just as Nemo and his new aquarium friends stage a daring escape! Gill, the leader of the Tank Gang, helps Nemo make his way to the spit sink because "all drains lead to the ocean." As he flips and flops his way to safety, look around for all these other toothy things!

Exam gloves

A set of teeth

A set of X-rays

Dental floss

Toothpaste

A toothbrush

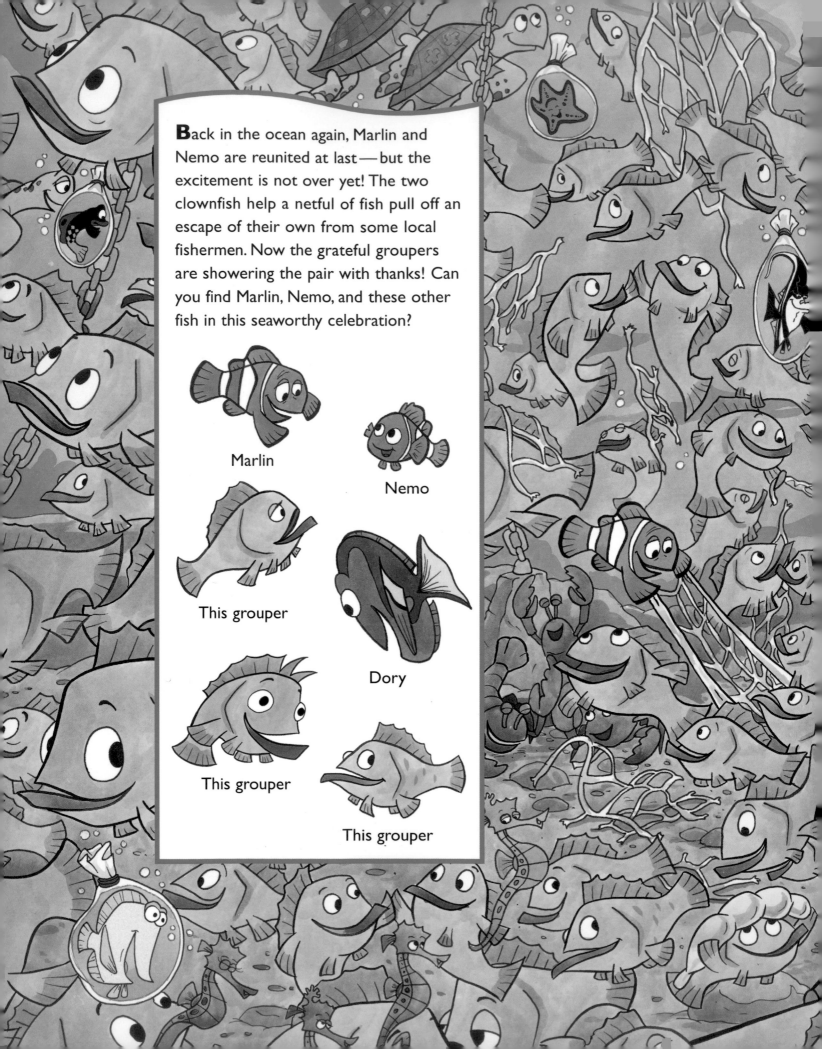

Back in the ocean again, Marlin and Nemo are reunited at last—but the excitement is not over yet! The two clownfish help a netful of fish pull off an escape of their own from some local fishermen. Now the grateful groupers are showering the pair with thanks! Can you find Marlin, Nemo, and these other fish in this seaworthy celebration?

Marlin

Nemo

This grouper

Dory

This grouper

This grouper

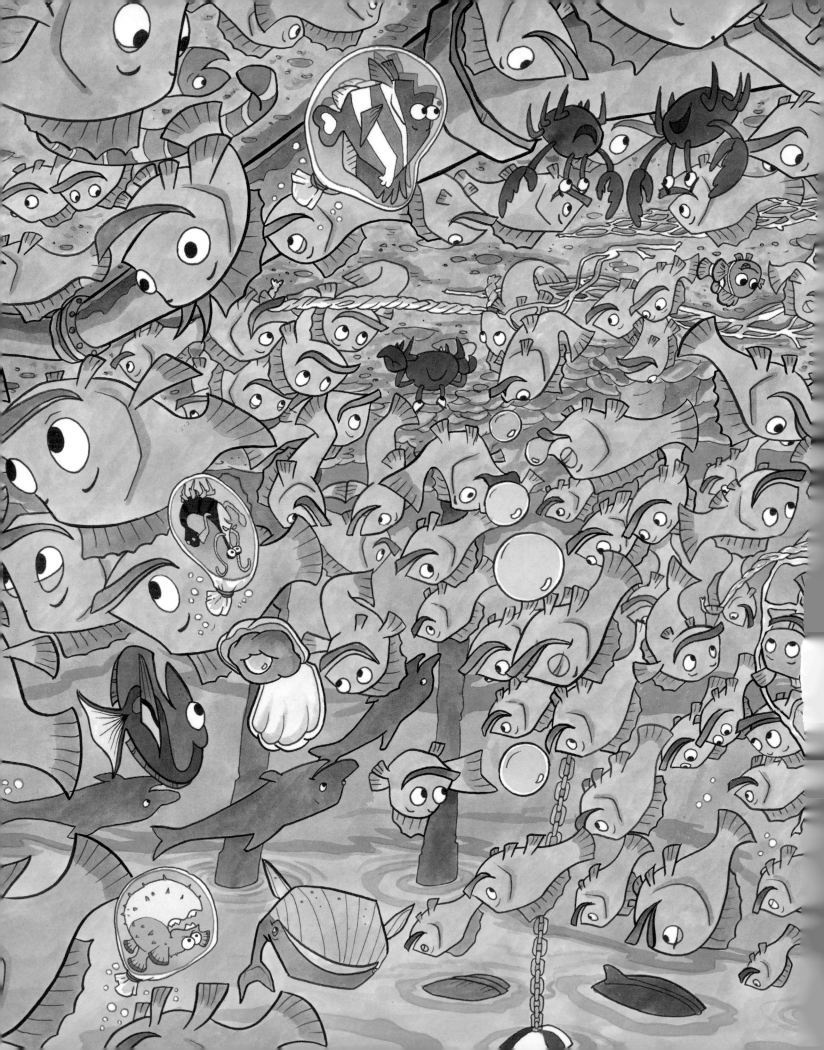

Swim on back to the reef to find these school-related things:

❏ jar of squid ink
❏ stones in the shape of pluses and minuses
❏ seaweed macrame
❏ algae map of Australia

Peach, the starfish, gets really bored with her face up against the tank glass all day. Can you count how many of these things she can see in the dentist's waiting room?

____ flowers on the wallpaper
____ stuffed animals
____ seashells
____ toothbrushes
____ cans of fish food

Go back to the submarine with Bruce and his vegetarian friends. Over the years, many divers have tried to explore the sunken sub, but for some reason they can't get out of there fast enough! Can you spot the things the divers left behind?

❏ diver's fin
❏ diver's mask
❏ underwater flashlight
❏ weight belt
❏ scuba tank
❏ underwater camera

Those helpful moonfish have even more great impressions than the ones they showed Marlin and Dory. Can you find these, too?

❏ "anchor"
❏ "sailboat"
❏ "diver"
❏ "arrow"
❏ "pirate flag"
❏ "life preserver"

Go back to the jellyfish forest. If you look closely, some of the jellies look different from the rest. Can you spot these strangely familiar jellyfish?

❏ a moon jelly
❏ a jelly fish
❏ a jelly roll
❏ a peanut-butter-and-jellyfish
❏ a jelly mold
❏ a strawberry jelly